ANiMAL HELPERS

Text by Štěpánka Sekaninová
Illustrations by Misha Bera

Albatros

CONTENT

1 DOGS

It barks, yaps, nuzzles, wags its tail when happy, cuddles, and shows love by licking its master or mistress all over with its pink, wet tongue. Whom do we mean? Well, the dog of, course! For us, people, dogs make faithful, lifelong friends. Indeed, the first tamed wolves walked at the side of prehistoric hunters 35,000 years ago.

With dogs, it's always fun!

WE'RE USEFUL

"That's right, we're useful." If a chorus of dogs were to bark this from dawn till dusk, it would be the absolute truth! Even the very first dogs helped humans to guard their homes and flocks of sheep and hunt game. They have always been wherever people have needed them.

iS iT A WOLF? iS iT A DOG? OR iS iT SOMETHiNG iN BETWEEN?

Here's the thing: the first household pets and people's helpers were wolves, the distant ancestors of today's dogs. As time went by, by various genetic mutations, these wolves became dogs. Unlike their doggy descendants, wolves are exclusively carnivorous, as a wolf's digestive tract can process nothing but meat. On the other hand, a hungry dog won't turn its nose up at a bowl of pasta or potatoes. This is the main difference between the wolf and the dog.

wolf

woof-woof

DOGS AS HUNTERS

Humans have always needed to provide themselves with food. In the past, what they didn't grow, they hunted. And with a clever dog at their side, hunting was a piece of cake. That's right—dogs, too, have performed the role of the hunter since time immemorial. What help does a hunting dog give? Well, it follows a wild animal's trail, drives it from its hiding place, attracts the attention of its master and, last but not least, retrieves the catch, delivering it to the master's feet.

> Hunting dogs need a highly developed sense of smell, good temperament, agility, speed, and willingness to work.

Stay with me, and I will feed you!

DOGS AS GUARDS

On hearing the word "dog," most people think of the words "friend," and "guard." As one of the first tasks humans gave their four-legged friends was the guarding of their property and land, this is hardly surprising. Dogs did this by barking loudly, thus making their presence known far and wide, and sometimes, by attacking intruders. From a Babylonian bas-relief from 2,200 BCE, on which one of the first guard dogs is immortalized, we know that dogs have been working as guards for centuries.

> Mosaics surviving from Pompeii provide clear evidence that in ancient Rome, it was quite normal to have a guard dog.

1 DOGS

TYPES OF HUNTING DOGS

A burrow specialist, the **terrier** is brilliant at sniffing out foxes and other creatures that live underground.

Guided by the scent of blood, the **scent hound** reliably tracks down wounded prey.

The **retriever** enjoys bringing hunted prey to its master's feet.

This is a typical stance, by which the dog alerts the hunter of the presence of nearby prey.

dog with prey

DOGS AS HERDERS

Those of our ancestors who preferred breeding sheep or cattle to hunting would have struggled to manage without a herding dog. Such a dog would protect its herd or flock from dangerous predators, wild stray dogs, and even thieves. It is probable that herding dogs were first used in ancient Mesopotamia, where the breeding of farm animals was common and widespread. Shepherd and drover dogs could manage a herd or flock without any human assistance as they moved from place to place, sometimes over great distances.

POSTAL DOGS

As the First World War raged on, bullets flew back and forth and the air was polluted with poison gas. A report pleading for assistance needed to be delivered. But it was unthinkable that a military postman should cover over four miles in that hell: he would surely die on the way. But what a human can't manage is easy-peasy for a dog. So it happened that the war created postal dogs, dogs large and small that scooted to their destination with an important message in a waterproof container attached to their collar, getting there in time to deliver news that could save human lives. Not even polluted surroundings held them back: with a special gas mask on, they were ready to go! The first postal dogs were found in ancient Rome, where they carried important messages in their stomachs. They would swallow a copper tube containing a folded note before dashing off to another camp. Sadly, the dog would pay for this message—which might have gone on to save many warriors—with its life. On arrival, it would be killed and disembowelled, so that the commander could get at the copper tube. The ancient world was a cruel place.

Herder dogs should bark often and loud, with gusto. When keeping a flock of sheep together, proper barking is a must.

1 DOGS

WORKING DOGS

As the years passed, humans' most faithful friend came to provide ever more services. Dogs could do so much more than just guard and hunt! Police officers appreciate a clever dog at their side—a dog that will obey their every word, be their faithful protector, detect explosives, and track down drugs, thieves, and other rogues. Such specially trained dogs are known as working dogs. As well as serving the police, working dogs help customs officials too.

I smell something . . . somebody's lying here under the rubble!

Lead dogs steer the team and set the pace. They must also be able to find a trail in bad conditions.

lead dog

DOG RESCUERS

In the First World War, many soldiers were wounded. And who helped their friends search for lost comrades on the battlefield? Well, dogs, of course! They came to serve yet another function—that of dog rescuers. The Second World War was even tougher. Bombarded cities fell like houses of cards. "Let's use dogs!" people cried, and their clever four-legged friends rescued unfortunate citizens from the rubble. Since the last world war, people have used the services of dogs in the mountains; having succeeded in tracking down people in the ruins of buildings, sniffer dogs have no difficulty in rescuing tourists trapped by an avalanche.

SLED DOGS AND MUSHERS

Dogs have been helping people pull sleds for 4,000 years. In regions with harsh conditions all year round, archaeologists still find in the snow remnants of the first sleds to which dogs were harnessed. The heavier and bulkier the sled's load, the greater the number of dogs needed to pull it. At the end of the 19th century, there was a sudden rush for gold in the harsh conditions of Alaska. As the search for gold nuggets was often boring, prospectors competed against one another with their packs of dogs, thus inventing a new sport known as mushing.

Dogs that can become sled dogs: Alaskan Malamutes, Siberian Huskies, and Greeland Dogs—all of them have robust constitutions, are good-natured, and like to pull.

Sled dogs help people in the polar regions carry heavy loads.

musher

sled

The two dogs behind the leader are called swing dogs—they help "swing" the team at turns.

swing dogs

wheel dogs

Wheel dogs must have a calm temperament. They pull the sled and navigate around trees or tight curves.

1 DOGS

HEARING DOGS

Did you know that dogs can help deaf people, too? Known as hearing dogs, these clever creatures can alert their master about many things, such as when someone is calling them, their telephone or alarm clock is ringing, or their microwave oven is beeping.
A hearing dog is so clever that if the deaf person were to drop their wallet without realizing, the dog would pick it up and put it into their hand.

YUMMY, TRUFFLES . . .

When hearing about the hunting of truffles, one of the world's greatest delicacies, most people think of pigs. Thanks to their refined sense of smell, pigs make excellent truffle hunters. However, as these omnivorous animals never pass up food, they might eat the delicious truffles before their handler realizes what is happening. In this regard, dogs are different: they seek out the truffles, bark, and wait, without taking a single bite. In the future, the only truffle hunter will be human's age-old friend, the dog.

You are my beloved white furry ball.

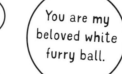

Truffles can be perfectly hidden, and a dog will still find them.

THERE'S NOTHING LIKE A DOG'S LOVE

As if all these abilities weren't enough, dogs can also help improve the mood of old and sick people and people with mental disabilities. Hugging a loving creature is a very special thing, and dogs are certainly loving. Experts call this kind of help canistherapy (therapy with dogs), and, believe it or not, this kind of supportive care has many benefits.

WHEN WAR iS RAGiNG

Humans have always fought and made war. And they have also dragged their faithful, four-legged friends into their messes. What wise creatures humans are! Fighting dogs have accompanied warriors on their campaigns since the dawn of human history. As well as guarding military camps, when called upon to fight, they tore their masters' adversaries to pieces, launching themselves at every enemy that crossed their path, and hunted wild animals to provide meat for the soldiers; in later times, they carried ammunition, sniffed out mines, and gave their soldiers great emotional support.

ASSiSTANCE DOG

An assistance dog helps a person who has a disability. It is common for an assistance dog to accompany a blind person—such a dog is known as a guide dog. But if you think that the guide dog is a convenience of modern times, think again—the first known depiction of a blind man with a dog to show him the way comes from 13th century China. In the First World War, many soldiers were blinded by shrapnel; the development of an assistance-dog service was a great help to them.

> A skillful assistance dog should be able to seek out doors, steps, pavements, crossings, benches, public transport stops, and shop counters. They should also recognize obstacles, stop well ahead of them, and lead the person around them. Last, the assistance dog knows how to lead a person across the road, turn left or right, and travel by public transport.

2 ELEPHANTS

Depending on its mood, it will trumpet, bellow, wave and beat its enormous ears, or spout water from its trunk. That's right—in this chapter, we will discuss the giant pachyderm called the elephant. But you may not know that this apparently clumsy animal has been helping humanity since time immemorial and continues to do so.

AS WHITE AS SNOW

To this day, white elephants are considered sacred in Thailand, as they are said to ensure prosperity on Earth. The more such elephants a monarch owns, the better his kingdom will fare. The sacred white elephant has never been put to work or made to fight.

DOMESTICATING ELEPHANTS

Although elephants are great helpers of humankind, we have never succeeded in fully domesticating and taming them, unlike horses, dogs, and cats. Maybe this is because these large mammals become irritable and aggressive during the breeding season, posing a danger to life.

Elephants are stubborn and hard to tame.

WORKING ELEPHANTS

The huge, mighty elephant can get a lot of important work done—in agriculture and construction (for instance, at the sawmill). It can lift with ease a load of nearly half a ton, and it can pull a load of one and a half tons. Elephants are not only good for heavy work: because of their patient nature, female elephants can manage more precise work too—such as placing tree trunks under a saw, arranging sawn wood in neat piles, and blowing away sawdust.

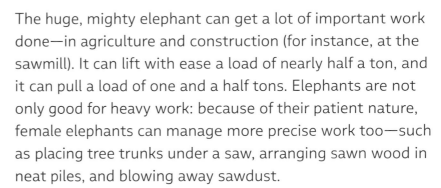

Monday, Tuesday, Wednesday . . . Every day is work!

Elephants have been helping humans since the begining of times.

SACRED ELEPHANTS

Elephants have an important position in the Buddhist religion, most notably in Asia. Legend has it that Queen Maya once had a strange dream, in which a white elephant entered her womb through her right side. Shortly thereafter, she conceived her son, the Buddha. The dream spoke to the queen in symbols, telling her to prepare to give birth to an exceptional man.

2 ELEPHANTS

IMPROVING THE FIGHT

As time passed and humans' techniques of war and combat improved, elephants came to carry a veritable tower on their backs, and this tower was filled with archers. When great numbers of thus equipped aggressive male elephants (only males were used in battle) were let loose on the enemy, the result was absolute mayhem. Opposing infantry and cavalry alike were overpowered in no time. Confronted by enraged elephants, horses would bolt.

WAR ELEPHANTS

Elephants have been great helpers of humans in battles and wars. Just imagine being confronted by such a colossus on the battlefield! Once it gets up a head of steam, it's like an animal tank! The easiest way to get out of this pickle is to run. Elephants first fought alongside humans in the 6th century BCE. Each elephant had an experienced guide on its back called a mahout, who controlled the creature with a special pole with a hook on the end, pressure applied by their feet, and the use of their voice.

THE GOD GANESHA

Ganesha is one of the most highly revered Hindu gods. A young man with a rounded belly, an elephant's head, and four arms, he is the god of wisdom, new beginnings, and prosperity and an important remover of obstacles on our life's journey.

TAKING US HERE, THERE, AND EVERYWHERE

Before trains and cars became widespread, in many Asian countries, elephants were a common means of transport for many people. These days, elephant transport serves as a tourist attraction.

ELEPHANTS APPROACHING RETIREMENT

In the battle against Alexander the Great, King Darius I of Persia used fifteen war elephants. The famous Hannibal crossed the Alps with 37 war elephants, and it was thanks to them that he eventually prevailed over the Romans. By the time of the First World War, in the 20th century, elephants were no longer used in battle; because of their extraordinary strength and resilience, they served as draft animals, for the transporting of extra-heavy loads.

In the past, elephants were used as useful vehicles; nowadays, riding them is just for fun.

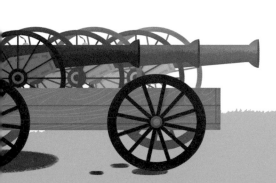

3 CATS

They miaow, purr, nuzzle up, cuddle, and stretch. Who are they? Well, cats, of course! Also known as pussies and kitties. Cats, too, are age-old friends of humans. But they certainly aren't as loyal to us as dogs. There's no chance that a cat would obey our every command! Archaeological digs in the Middle East discovered evidence of cats around human dwellings as long ago as 10,000 BCE.

Where there is a mouse, there is a cat.

HELP, A MOUSE!

"Help, a mouse! It will eat our crops!" Around 8,000 BCE, the first farmers may well have been startled into shouting such words. Through agriculture, they tried to prove that it was better to grow grain than to spend all day, every day chasing around the forest, hunting game. The problem was, it seemed that no one had reckoned with the greedy mice. Then, a predator—the cat—arrived on the scene and set about getting rid of the troublesome rodents. As a result, grateful farmers made friends with the elegant mice-hunters, feeding and stroking them in return for the protection of the full granaries from mice. Before long, wild cats were setting up home near human dwellings.

CATS AND THE GLORIOUS EGYPTIAN EMPIRE

The people of ancient Egypt loved their cats, and for good reason: as well as protecting their crops from mice and other rodents, cats would hunt and exterminate different pests—Egypt was home to poisonous snakes, including cobras and vipers, and scorpions. Egyptian cats may have been regularly fed delicacies, but did they earn them!

CATS AND HUMANS GO HUNTING

Everyone knows that humans brought along dogs when hunting. In Egypt, keen hunters took their cats out hunting. Just imagine! We know this from archaeological finds. Dating back to ancient times, these depict fishermen and bird hunters with cats at their side. The cats were too free-thinking to retrieve the catch, of course; their job was probably scaring birds out of their nests, which were hidden in dense growths of papyrus. But that kind of help is useful too, right?

CAT, CAT! PROTECT ME!

Because cats protected humans from dangerous reptiles, as time passed, they took on an important role in the religion of the Egyptians. Indeed, the cat became a symbol of protection. Women in particular—both alive and in their tombs—wore a great many amulets depicting cats as protection against the sting of the scorpion and the bite of the snake and in support of their fertility in this world and the next.

Help me! I'm really afraid of cats!

Cats protected humans not only from rodents but also snakes and scorpions.

3 CATS

cat

OTHER IMPORTANT ROLES FOR CATS

Egypt wasn't the only place to hold the cat in high esteem. In China, this free-spirited creature found shelter in Buddhist temples; in return, it would protect the land from poverty. In Japan, cats were vigilant guards against the dangers posed by rats—they watched over the cocoons of silkworms and valuable manuscripts kept in temples.

HER DIVINE MAJESTY

So high was the esteem in which the ancient Egyptians held their cats that they even turned the cat into a goddess. Named Bastet, it was her task to protect the people of Egypt. She had a beautiful cat's head on a woman's body.

The splendid cat goddess Bastet was popular not only among poor people but also among Pharaohs.

Bastet was originally portrayed as a lioness.

MiAOW! A MESSAGE FOR A GOD

In ancient Egypt, cats often lived in a temple, where their nimble shoulders had a very important load to bear. They were assigned the task of communicating with the gods. Unhappy souls with important messages for or requests of a god would enter the temple and order the killing of one of the sacred cats, in the belief that the god would show mercy for the sacrifice. And maybe they did. Who knows?

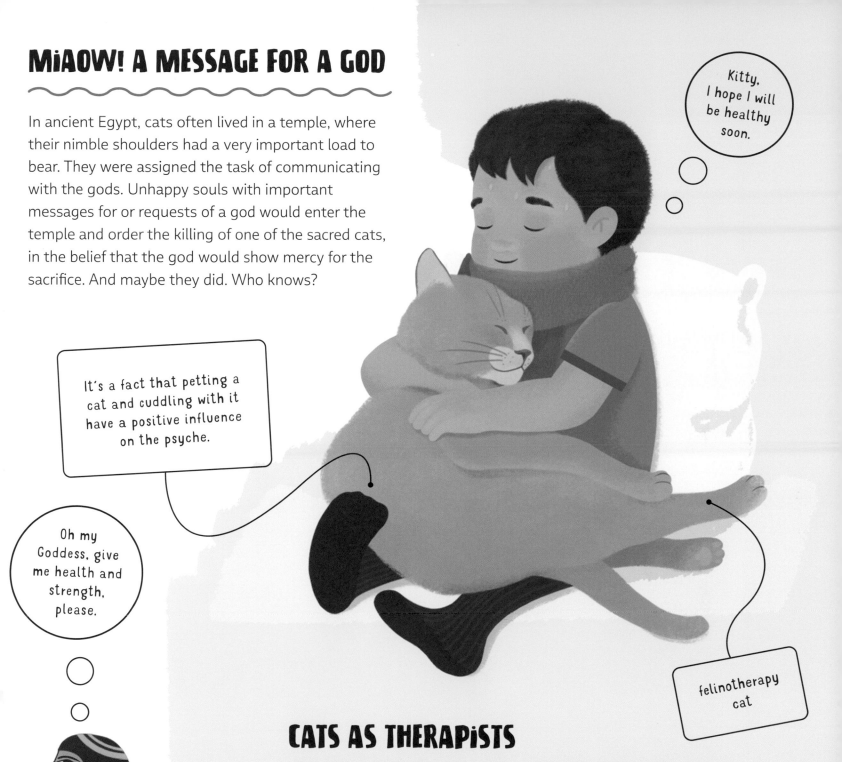

Kitty, I hope I will be healthy soon.

It's a fact that petting a cat and cuddling with it have a positive influence on the psyche.

Oh my Goddess, give me health and strength, please.

felinotherapy cat

CATS AS THERAPISTS

Cats have bravely confronted snakes and rodents for many centuries. Today, they have other useful roles too. One is as a very effective therapist for work with elderly and sick people and with children. Therapist cats will allow themselves to be stroked, combed, and cuddled. "What's the big deal?" you may ask. Well, the combing of a cat's hair helps to get stiff joints moving, thus exercising fine motor skills in the hand. What's more, love and cuddles from a therapist cat provide lonely people with much-needed emotional warmth, making them feel better. Such help is really important.

4 PIGEONS

They coo, burble, and puff out their chests as they fly around the statues and buildings of towns. They can always be relied upon to find their way home safely. We are talking about pigeons and doves, who have been friends with humans for nearly 67,000 years. Yes, we can be that specific—archaeologists discovered that the very first breeders of pigeons were the Neanderthals.

Pigeons, fill your bellies!

dovecote

LET'S TAME A PIGEON!

There can be little doubt that the pigeon was one of the very first creatures to be tamed by humans. It happened in Mesopotamia and the Near East 6,000 years ago, at a time when agriculture was developing quite quickly. Pigeons were more than happy in the company of humans and their crop-filled fields. So much food for their beaks to feast on! Once pigeons exchanged their homes in rugged cliffs for human dwellings, an unbreakable friendship was established.

POST FLYING YOUR WAY

It didn't take humans long to notice and take full advantage of the pigeon's amazing sense of direction and love of home. And what did people use pigeons for? Well, for delivering important messages to allies some distance away. The first professional pigeon post birds went into service 2,500 years ago. In Egypt, for instance, pigeons carried messages from ships to make contact between cities. And in ancient Greece, they would set out to deliver the joyful news of an Olympic victory to the victor's home as soon as it happened.

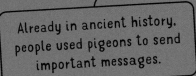
Already in ancient history, people used pigeons to send important messages.

pigeon

THANKS FOR MAKING ME RICH!

Without me, Rothschild wouldn't have become so rich.

In the days before mobile phones, ownership of a reliable postal pigeon was of great strategic importance. A certain banker called Mr. Rothschild was one such an owner. And how quick his pigeon was! After Napoleon's army was defeated at Waterloo in 1813, the bird promptly flew home with the important news. As a result, Mr. Rothschild knew the result of the battle three days before the British government did, and as any good financier would, he acted accordingly. He became very rich indeed. Sometimes, time is of the essence.

Banker Nathan Mayer Rothschild

4 PIGEONS

THE PIGEON AND THE FIRST NEWS AGENCY

Ordinary postal pigeons were present at the birth of the world's very first news agency, founded by Paul Julius Reuter. In 1848, Reuter left his native Germany for Paris, where he was employed by a press office, sending the latest news from the Bourse between Aachen and Brussels—by pigeon post. Today, the Reuters agency is based in London and it is one of the world's leading news agencies, for more than financial news.

HAVE YOU GOT ENOUGH FOR A PIGEON?

As the ancient Persians, Phoenicians, Greeks, and Romans were truly grateful for the services of postal pigeons, it's no wonder that such pigeons cost their owners a fortune. In later times, wealthy European nobles had dovecotes built on their estates, some of which housed 2,000 birds. Quite a demonstration of their prosperity and dominance!

pigeon

During the war, pigeons saved many humans lives.

PIGEONS IN WARTIME

Postal pigeons have done very important work during wartime. They have carried important messages and calls for help through raging gunfire. More than once, their work saved the lives of a whole regiment; in this regard, the actions of a bird called Cher Ami are well known. During the First World War, pigeons fitted with miniature cameras took shots of enemy camps, for instance.

Deliver my message in time, please.

THE INCREDIBLE PIGEON

Not only have pigeons helped human masters for thousands of years, but they can even keep people entertained. How? By racing each other, that's how! Specially trained birds compete in short- and long-distance races and even in marathons. And believe it or not, there are competitions for pigeon acrobats too. These birds may look ordinary, but, as you can see, their abilities are practically unlimited!

A PRICELESS PIGEON

As you can see, pigeons held their value even in wartime. After occupying Belgium in the Second World War, the seizing and emptying of the enemy's dovecotes was one of the first things the German army did; then, it used the trained pigeons to its own advantage. And the Second World War was not the last conflict in which pigeons were used. Even today, the Swiss army considers them the most reliable means of delivering a message in the difficult environment of the Alps.

Although an ordinary pigeon at first glance, it can actually do incredible stunts!

5 HORSES

They whinny, clop their hooves, stomp, trot, canter, and gallop, with or without a rider on their back. Whom do we mean? Well, horses, of course! Stallions, ponies, mares, and fillies alike. These noble animals were already friends with humans in 4,000 BCE. And believe it or not, the friendship between horse and human has changed history by leaps and bounds.

What a beautiful foal I have!

Here begins the shared story of people and horses.

THE HORSE AS VEHICLE

It is around 4,000 BCE, and horses and humans are already friends. In fact, they began to share a household about 2,000 years earlier. Not only is the horse humans' trusty companion, but also their able assistant. With a good horse, distances are shorter. Humans sit on a horse's back and travel on it for miles, to borders and beyond. Thanks to travel on horseback, the world suddenly became a smaller place.

Even before humans sat on horses' backs, they used their new companions to pull heavy loads. Later, of course, horses would become excellent means of transport.

SiGN OF PRESTiGE

To make the horse more effective, someone came up with the idea of putting it in a harness, hitching it to a cart or coach, and using it to move the whole family. Whoever had a horse was rich indeed: for many years, ownership of this excellent animal was a sign of prestige.

HORSE TRAiNS

"One family is too little," said one ever dissatisfied, ever busy man at the beginning of the 19th century. "We need something to carry the whole city, indeed the whole nation!" Bim, bam, and there it was—the horse-powered streetcar, the forerunner of the train, if you wish.

warhorse

WARHORSES

As we know, since ancient times, humans have waged so many wars that we might think they enjoyed it. When they teamed up with horses, their fierce battles became truly ferocious. Thanks to horses, humans became more mobile, enabling victorious warriors to occupy land and thus create ever larger territories for themselves. The first battles to be fought with horses took place in key provinces and cities of ancient times—India, Mesopotamia, Egypt, Greece, and Rome in particular. At first, horses pulled chariots containing men behind protective shields; later, warriors would tear into battle on horseback.

The best view is from the horse's saddle.

RIDING HEAVY VRSUS THE LIGHT HORSE

On the battlefield, horses lent any help they could. A knight on the back of a powerful steed, in heavy armor and armed to the teeth, became a symbol of medieval warfare. But over time, the heavily laden, less mobile knight gave way to the knight that preferred a so-called light horse—his body would be covered only partially, making movement easier. Before long, brigades of light horse made up much of an army and often decided the outcome of a battle.

Transporting heavy loads from one place to another was easy work for horses. Therefore, horses helped soldiers exhausted by war.

I wish the war was over!

light horse

FiRST WORLD WAR

Equestrian units, known as cavalries, played an important role in the fighting of the First World War. The methods of combat had changed by then; however, the effects of machine-gun fire and grenades were as catastrophic on horses as they were on their riders. For this reason, from the 1930s onward, the use of horses in combat was gradually abandoned. But horses continued to play an important role in wartime—they were used in the transportation of cargo to and from bomb-stricken railways.

HORSES AND AGRICULTURE

When we think of horses, we often think of fields and plows too. This is because these muscular creatures used to help humans with farming. They would plow and loosen the soil, assist in the sowing of crops, and, last but not least, pull the carts carrying the harvest back home. But if you were thinking that farmers relied on the help of horses from time immemorial, think again: in the distant past, the use of horses was a privilege enjoyed only by the nobility and the wealthy, for a horse cost a fortune. It took a long time for farmers to work their way up to the noble horse from the ox and the draft cow.

In the beginnings of agriculture, only cows and oxen plowed the soil. Over time, farmers also started using horses.

HORSES AND HUNTING

Horses aren't used only for fighting and hard work. From ancient times on, horses have been used for fun, too. Special riding horses were bred for the rigors of the hunt, in which hunters on horseback chased foxes, stags and other game to the sound of hunting horns.

There wasn't a single aristocrat without a noble horse in their stables.

Just a little bit closer . . . and you're mine!

Hunted game stood no chance against a horseback rider.

HORSES AND THE FOREST

The importance of the horse for agriculture can be compared with its importance for forestry. For a very long time, horses have gathered and transported timber, carried it away from hard-to-reach places, and distributed young trees for planting. The horse has the great advantage of being able to move with confidence through terrain that is difficult to cross. A horse chosen for work in the forest must be very mobile, agile, and hardworking, with a calm nature and a robust constitution.

horse

HORSES AND TOURNAMENTS

Most people today manage quite well without a horse, but this has not always been the case. Indeed, for princes, princesses, and knights, a horse was a must. Knights were men in armor that rode their horses off to war. Knights would also compete on their noble steeds in arenas, for the hearts of beautiful ladies. These knightly competitions were known as tournaments.

5 HORSES

HORSES FOR FUN

Friends make good helpers and even better companions. This is as true of horses as it is of humans. Sport is another area in which horses work to the benefit of humans. We're thinking here of horse racing, show jumping, and dressage (the performance of trained maneuvers). People like to compete on horseback, and they have done so since ancient times.

horse

HORSES AND HEALTH

Like the cat and the dog, the beautiful, light-stepping horse can exert a healing power on us, humans. Horse riding helps with the coordination of body movements, the stimulation of the central nervous system, and the improvement of posture and overall fitness. Additionally, the simple contact with the animal is good for human health on a psychological level. Quite simply, horses have long added an element of joy to our lives.

BEWARE OF THE HORSE

Native Americans could have attached a sign with these words to their corrals. People of aboriginal nations soon recognized the great intelligence of the splendid animal called the horse. They also noticed that horses could tell from a great distance whether the person approaching them had good or wicked intentions. Thanks to their horses, Native Americans could identify a coming danger in time to get out of its path.

Faster, run faster, horsey! It looks like we are winning.

Horses and Native Americans seem inseparable. But believe it or not, horses were not tamed by them until the 18th century.

Believe it or not, but a horse is as good as a dog when it comes to protection.

American Indian Horse

puma

6 DOLPHINS

They whistle, sing, and laugh—indeed, they love communication of all kinds. Humans have had a fascination with these merry sea- and ocean-going swimmers since ancient times. As our ancestors believed that a dolphin was a reincarnated god, it is hardly surprising that a much-revered Greek deity—Apollo, the god of the Sun—was dedicated to this creature.

You can become friends with dolphins!

Without dolphins, the crew of this shipwreck would perish in the sea.

sailor

COME AND STROKE ME

Dolphins enjoy human attention and like to be stroked. In the 1970s, several dolphins settled in Australia's Shark Bay, where they would literally reach out to curious human visitors—naturally, people were very keen to stroke them and throw fish into their mouths. As the kind and intelligent dolphins wished to be in no one's debt, they returned the favor by offering the humans fish they had caught.

rescuer

I promise to learn to swim before I go to the sea again.

HELP ME, I'M DROWNING!

We will perhaps never know for sure whether these sensational events truly happened. They were maybe produced by the vivid imaginations of ancient chroniclers. But we know for sure that in recent times, dolphins used their bodies to push a drowning swimmer into shallow waters.

TRUE OR FALSE?

Sources from antiquity tell us that these friendly, charming creatures saved ship-wrecked, drowning sailors and seafarers more than once, teaming up to carry them ashore and drive away blood-thirsty sharks.

6 DOLPHiNS

THE WORLD'S BEST NAViGATORS

In the late 19th and early 20th centuries, a dolphin would swim alongside naval ships, accompanying them through dangerous waters, making their journey as smooth, fluent, and safe as possible. This dolphin became known as Jack. Every time sailors in the waters of New Zealand spotted Jack swimming up to their ship, they would be mightily relieved. Sadly, this super-intelligent animal died in 1903, after 40 years of loyal, voluntary service for humankind. He was killed by a shot from the gun of a drunken passenger.

LET'S BUILD UNDER THE SEA

So far, we've only talked about untrained dolphins. Specially trained ones help with underwater construction work by sending messages between ships and carrying on their backs injured workers in urgent need of help.

DOLPHiNS iN SERVICE

Incorrigible humanity thinks nothing of dragging a kind, friendly creature like the dolphin into its hostilities. An army of trained dolphins can be used to detect mines in parts of a ship that are underwater and to monitor the approach of hostile divers or submarines; dolphins are also trained to locate explosives that have been laid at sea.

BEWARE OF SHARKS!

Do you know how dolphins save swimmers from sharks? Well, they swim around the person in ever narrower circles, until the lurking predator loses interest in the prey or a lifeboat arrives to fish the poor human out.

FISHING WITH DOLPHINS

Friendly dolphins are naturally very fond of humans. We know this because they help fishermen lure fish into their nets. In return, the fishermen give the dolphins a part of the catch, and both parties end up satisfied. We're talking about ordinary dolphins in the wild, not trained ones. This happened in Brazil.

DOLPHIN THERAPY

They are very good at recognizing the client's state of mind and treating them accordingly. As the patient plays with the dolphin—throwing and catching balls and riding on its back, for instance—they learn to accept the animal's love, thus regaining trust in themselves and the world around them.

7 CHEETAHS

They purr like cats, hiss, and spit. What they don't do is roar menacingly. In any case, they are much-feared hunters who chase, catch up with, and seize antelopes. That's right—there is no one faster than the cheetah. According to the latest research, the cheetah took its beautiful spots to its North African homeland over 100,000 years ago.

They get tired quickly, but can develop a speed up to 75 miles per hour!

AS FAST AS THE WIND!

The super-elegant cheetah can reach a speed of 75 miles per hour—when it is truly hungry and the dash is no more than 1,000 feet. If it were to go any further at top speed, its body would begin to overheat.

THE CHEETAH AS A DOMESTICATED HUNTER

Archaeologists have more than once found the mummy of a cheetah in the tomb of a pharaoh. In ancient Egypt, tamed cheetahs lived at the royal court. Not only were they lovable pets, but also helped a lot with hunting antelopes and gazelles. Because of their expertise, cheetahs joined on hunts in India, Persia, Turkey, China, and Hungary.

A CAT WITH A DOG'S NATURE

Although cheetahs are felines, they are built more like dogs than cats. They are also more like dogs in their nature, which allows them to get close to humans. An experienced breeder will manage to tame these fleet-footed beasts, teaching them to respond to up to twenty commands. So next time you meet someone walking a cheetah on a lead, don't be surprised.

WHY ARE CHEETAHS SO FAST?

These wild cats are so phenomenally fast due to their flexible spine and their claws, which are unable to retract, unlike those of other felines. These permanently drawn claws give the cheetah the advantage the spikes on the soles of running shoes give an athlete. Add to this a long tail to act as a rudder, and it's no wonder the cheetah is a champion sprinter.

HO'/ THE HUI'T '/A: DOI'E

Tame cheetahs specially trained for the hunt would be transported on special carts or on horse-back to areas where antelopes and gazelles were known to graze. All that remained for their human companions to do was to release them at the right time. The highly excited animals would set off at lightning speed; before the poor herbivores knew what was happening, they would be lying on the ground. Having moved in quickly for the kill, the human hunters would reward their animal helpers with the catch's fresh blood and guts.

Nobody will escape me!

Akbar The Great had the body of a man but the soul of the greatest cheetah in Indian history.

ASiA

Ancient Egyptians weren't the only ones to keep cuddly cheetahs at the royal court—wealthy Asian rulers and Indian maharajahs did so too. Two such examples are the Mongolian tyrant ruler Genghis Khan and the 16th-century Indian ruler Akbar the Great. The latter thought pretty big—up to 1,000 cheetahs could be found at his court.

CHEETAH VERSUS HYENA

If cheetahs were able to reproduce in captivity, maybe we would have succeeded in domesticating them as we domesticated the dog. In the distant past, humans attempted to domesticate the hyena, which—in evolutionary terms—is more like a dog than a cat. The ancient Egyptians often kept spotted hyenas, sending them on the hunt alongside dogs. But as hard as they tried, humans never managed to tame these beasts permanently.

WELCOME TO EUROPE

The reputation of these brilliant hunters spread to Europe in the 5th century. From then on, European rulers and great blue bloods were assisted by cheetahs, many of which they received as gifts from the Ottoman Empire. The presence of cheetahs on the hunt would have come as no surprise to anyone visiting medieval Italy, France, or England. In India, cheetahs were still used for hunting in the early 20th century.

8 COWS

It moos, provides milk, and looks at humans with big, honest, lovely eyes. Today, it is a gentle, calm creature—no one would dream of being afraid of it. After all, it's had lots of time to get used to humans—8,000 years, to be exact. What are we talking about? Well, Bos taurus, the cow, of course! The cow was one of the very first animals to be domesticated by humans.

MY WILD ANCESTOR

But don't think that taming the cow 8,000 years ago was an easy matter. In those days, the cows that ran about the meadows were aurochs, the wild ancestors of the cows of today. The aurochs was almost six and a half feet in height, strong as an ox, and armed with a large, menacing pair of curved horns. In their ongoing search for pastures new, the nomadic shepherds of those times took their lives into their hands in trying to tame the aurochs—yes, that's how dangerous the ancestor of the cow was!

Tame me if you can but it won't be easy!

END OF THE AUROCHS

Although the aurochs was a truly terri-fying animal, over time, our ancestors succeeded in taming it. By doing so, they launched humanity into a new orbit, where further progress could be achieved. Not only did the cow become the first draft animal, but also the first animal to be ridden, making distant places much easier to reach. No, we're not mistaken—people in Africa really did ride cows before they got around to taming horses.

It's a wonderful view from the cow's back!

It doesn't look like it, but even a cow can be ridden like a horse.

DRAUGHT COWS

Cows, bulls, and oxen are so strong that they can pull loads of several tons; they can also drag a plow across a field. Very often, cows, bulls, and oxen were yoked in pairs, side by side or one in front of the other; they were in the charge of a so-called drover. Although slower and more easily tired than the horse, the cow has made a great contribution to humankind's economic progress.

8 COWS

THE COW AND RELIGION

When we hear the word "bull," we think of something enormously strong. It will come as no surprise to learn that the ancient Egyptians took the bull as a symbol of strength and fertility. The pharaohs, who longed to possess at least a little of the bull's greatness, took titles such as "Mighty bull" and "Bull among the stars." Meanwhile, the goddess Hathor was often depicted as a cow, a source of milk rich in fat.

BULL iSLAND

Crete was so keen on the bull, it became the central figure in this Greek island's Minoan civilization. Here, too, the bull was a symbol of strength, fertility, and abundant harvest. Bulls would be sacrificed on important Cretan occasions, and special bull tournaments would be held, during which people would ride on bulls and jump from one animal to another. Such events symbolized the process of taming these super-strong creatures.

sacred cow

BARBELL OR COW?

It may be difficult to believe, but in ancient Greece, the cow was used as a weight for lifting. A strongman and many-time Olympic champion called Milo of Croton would train for a wrestling match by carrying a cow on his shoulders. It's no wonder that Milo was unbeatable—an adult cow weighs up to one ton.

Instead of dumbbells, Greek athletes simply picked up a cow.

Jump over a running bull

I am so hungry! Where is my food?

THE MINOTAUR—THE BEST KNOWN BULL OF ALL

Further evidence of the close connection of the cow/bull and the island of Crete is found in Greek mythology. The story goes that the wife of the Cretan king Minos fell in love with a white bull and bore him a son—a monster with the body of a human and the head of a bull. The Minotaur (so the love child was named) was imprisoned by Minos in a labyrinth, to which every nine years, seven Athenian maidens and seven Athenian youths would be sent.

9 PiGS

domestic pigs

It grunts, squeals, and gobbles up every scrap of food it comes across. Whom else can we be talking about but the adaptable, amiable, highly sociable domestic pig, a faithful companion of humankind over many years. The pig was one of the first animals to be domesticated by humans.

LONG AND YET LONGER AGO

People in southern Europe, the region around the Baltic Sea, and eastern Asia began to adapt the wild pig to their own way of life sometime between 7,000 BCE and 4,000 BCE. This coincided with the time when our ancestors gave up their lives as hunter-gatherers for the relatively settled lives of farmers.

wild boar

WHY THE PIG?

As pigs ate whatever they came across, they gobbled up all the leftovers, clearing up waste, and leaving everything around the house spick-and-span, keeping their human companions happy. What's more, pigs reproduced quickly, thus increasing the wealth of their owners—the more pigs in the yard, the more prosperous the farmer. In short, pigs were really important. In the 9th century BCE, the Franks calculated the area of a woodland by the number of pigs that fed from it.

One day, I will weigh over 600 lbs!

PIGS AND MYTHOLOGY

While humans have raised many domesticated and untamed animals to sacred status, their attitude toward the pig has always been full of contradictions. On one hand, people admired the pig for its strength and fearlessness; on the other, they feared it, as an enraged boar would lay waste to everything in its path.

I'm an omnivore and you will not save the garden from me!

9 PiGS

ANYONE FOR ROAST PORK?

Every Christmas, the people of Denmark and Sweden eat a traditional sweetbread in the shape of a boar. This is because in these countries, pigs represent the spirit of grain, which protects fields and crops.

This is the spirit of grain!

You can see the colors of the Danish and Swedish flags. Which colors belong to which country?

猪

iN THE SiGN OF THE BOAR

While in most places in the world, pigs lost their leading position in human households to goats and sheep, in China, pigs went from strength to strength. Not for nothing is the pig included in the Chinese horoscope, and given these characteristics: honesty, trustfulness, candor, and lack of guile.

¡ SMELL DELICIOUS TRUFFLES!

Did you know that pigs have a brilliant sense of smell? Because they have always searched for food in the ground, they are able to sniff out anything edible, even if it lies ten feet deep in the ground. In the past, pigs were truffle hunters of the highest reputation. Truffles are delicious fungi that grow next to tree roots, at depths of between 11 inches and 6.5 feet. But there was a problem with porcine truffle hunters—they, too, loved the taste of truffles and would often eat their find before their human companions knew what was happening.

The Nile cross, or "ankh," depicts life earthly and eternal.

EGYPT

A good example of this double-standard view of the pig is from ancient Egypt. Set, the god of the desert, transformed into a boar before killing his brother Osiris, the god of vegetation. Set was also in pig form when he wounded Osiris' son, Horus. In Egypt, the pig was a symbol of evil.

10 GEESE

Birds of a feather flock together. And these honk and hiss as they protect their own; it's enough to make anyone afraid. These intrepid creatures are domestic geese. Today, we, humans, think of geese as useful creatures because of their delicious meat and soft down feathers. But our ancestors had a deeper appreciation of geese; in fact, they considered them to be sacred creatures, dedicated to individual gods.

A wild goose can weigh a maximum of 11 lbs.

WHO FIRST TAMED THE GOOSE?

The domestication of the goose probably began around 5,000 BCE, in Mesopotamia. In the 2nd and 3rd millennia BCE, the ancient Egyptians, Greeks, and Europeans began to breed these white-winged birds in abundance. At that time, the Chinese preferred the swan. The goose earned the affection of humans by the fact that newly hatched chicks treated them like replacement parents.

A goose egg is at least 2 times larger than a chicken egg. It weighs about 7 oz.

EGYPTIAN GOOSE

In contrast, the domestic goose can weigh up to 29 lbs.

While the Chinese domesticated the long-necked swan, the Egyptians favored the goose, granting it untouchable status by dedicating it to the goddess Isis, patron of the pharaohs. As a result, geese would run about their temples, honking loudly at any perceived danger; they would be part of a pharaoh's company, as favorite pets. Geb, the god of the earth and crops and father of the goddess Isis, was depicted with a beautiful goose on his head.

Guard goose #42 at your service!

A noble man with his goose.

GOOSEY GOOSEY GANDER, WHITHER SHALL I WANDER?

If you were thinking that geese are stupid creatures that couldn't care a fig about who looks after them and feeds them, think again. Geese can recognize the voices of their owners. Call a goose and it will separate from its flock by the pond and obey the summons immediately, following you to the end of the world if you so demanded. In ancient Rome, it was not unusual for an aristocrat to walk around with a faithful goose at their heels, just like walking with a dog today.

10 GEESE

THE GEESE OF THE CAPITOLINE HILL

It is said of geese that they make great guards—even better than dogs. Legend has it that in 387 BCE, the goose guards of the Capitoline Hill in Rome saved it from being conquered. This was the time when the Gauls, commanded by Brennus, sacked the city. All that remained to be captured was the fortified Capitoline, which Roman soldiers were defending tooth and nail. The Gauls planned to surprise and defeat the defenders at night. Luckily, the temple of the goddess Juno was home to a flock of geese, whose loud honking announced the attack so that the Capitoline could be defended.

ANTIQUITY

The ancient Greeks, too, held the honking goose in high regard. They depicted Aphrodite, the goddess of love, riding a goose. The goose was also the symbol of Persephone, the wife of Hades, the god of the underworld.

Roman soldiers

Brennus—the Gallic leader

HOW ABOUT SOME WEEDING?

How difficult it must be to be the owner of a large cotton plantation, which needs to be weeded every day! The sun beats down, your body aches, yet your work seems to make hardly any difference; no sooner have you finished weeding on one side than you must begin again on the other. But then the answer comes along, in the form of the chatterbox goose. That's right, these aquatic birds can help here, too—with their beaks, by pecking out all the unwanted plants. What's more, they are glad to do it. Yum! They ignore cotton, as they don't like its taste.

BEWARE OF THE GOOSE!

Geese have proven themselves to be excellent guards throughout history and all over the world. This includes the wartime. For instance, the British army used geese as vigilant protectors in its fight against the Japanese. Today, geese keep a lookout for intruders at one of Scotland's most famous distilleries. The distillery's owners can rest assured that as long as the geese remain, they won't lose a drop of whisky, still less a whole bottle.

GOOSE LOYALTY

We would do well to follow the example of the ordinary goose. Having chosen his mate, the gander lives with her until they are parted by death. What's more, they care for and protect their young together.

Woe to the vanquished!

11 CAMELS

A camel's humps do not hold water!

Camels can withstand high temperatures other creatures cannot. They can work for a long time without water, and they are more than modest in their dietary needs—they will happily munch on tough, poor-quality plants accustomed to long periods of drought. Known as the Ship of the Desert, the trusty camel—both the single-humped and two-humped species—has provided humankind with an irreplaceable service for thousands of years.

Arabian camels have only one hump, while Asian camels have two.

WHY DOESN'T YOUR PURSE JINGLE?

But why should it? In the distant past, people in the Middle East paid with camels, not money. Taxes, tolls, and many other important things were paid for with a predetermined number of camels. Later, pictures of camels were engraved on coins—perhaps as a reminder of times when merchants paid for goods not with coins but with dromedaries.

HUMANS AND CAMELS

Humans first tamed camels over 5,000 years ago, in the lands of Arabia. Many years later, the perennial Ship of the Desert appeared in Africa, where it settled contentedly among the nomadic peoples, moving them from place to place with great dedication and patience.

Holy goodness!

The first recorded use of the camel as a military animal was by the Arab king Gindibu in 853 BCE.

CAMELS AT WAR

Like the elephant and the dog, people took the camel into the din of battle. In terrible conditions, camels would pull heavy equipment and transport fighting men from place to place and wounded men away from the battle. When camel riders came into conflict with cavalry on horseback, the camels nearly always won. Horses were petrified of camels—just as they were of elephants—and would run away from them in panic.

HOW MANY CAMELS DO YOU HAVE?

At the time when camels were faithful life companions for no-madic peoples, they were very valuable. In fact, a person's status in society was determined by how many Ships of the Desert they had. The more camels in the herd, the better off the family.

11 CAMELS

A GROOM'S GIFT

In the past, when a young man in Arabia found a beautiful girl to marry, he would have to prove his love and ability to care for her with a payment of some kind, known as a "mahr." What do you think he gave her? You've guessed it—a camel, or maybe several.

The little one is so cute!

LOAD UP THE CAMEL!

Merchant caravans of endless length make their way through the desert—slowly, under the scorching sun. Every day, another 25 miles to go. Bad weather doesn't faze them: whatever the conditions, they are able to carry a heavy load, human or otherwise, and pull a special cart. A camel wasn't just a means of payment—it was an important means of transportation, too. Unlike the horse and the donkey, it could climb dunes of fine sand without falling.

Camels can completely shut their nostrils during sandstorms.

CAMEL RACING

Since time immemorial, besides working with humans, camels have also entertained them. But it may surprise you to learn that in countries of the Middle East, where there are Ships of the Desert aplenty, camel races have been held for thousands of years. The descendants of the nomadic Bedouins who started these races are today's wealthy sheikhs. In the past, the riders were ultra-light boys aged about six years; today, the camels are ridden by robot jockeys.

CAMELS AND TOURISM

Visit Tunisia or Egypt during your holidays and perhaps you'll get the chance to discover for yourself what it's like to ride a camel. That's right, these tireless animals have become tourist attractions. And believe it or not, it's not so unusual to keep a camel as a house pet. A camel can be as cuddly and affectionate as a cat, and it is happy to obey commands.

Camels have three sets of eyelids and two rows of eyelashes to keep sand out of their eyes.

Camels have thick lips, which let them forage for thorny plants other animals can't eat.

ANIMAL HELPERS

© Designed by B4U Publishing for Albatros,
an imprint of Albatros Media Group, 2021.
Na Pankráci 30, Prague 4, Czech Republic
Author: Štěpánka Sekaninová
Illustrator: Misha Bera
Printed in Ukraine by KHBF Unisoft, LLC.
ISBN 978-80-00-05946-4